FAST FORWARD

Earthquakes
Through Time

Published in 2009 by The Rosen Publishing Group, Inc.
29 East 21st Street, New York, NY 10010

Created and produced by Nicholas Harris and Claire Aston,
Orpheus Books Ltd

U.S. editor: Kara Murray
Illustrator: Peter Dennis (*Linda Rogers Associates*)
Consultant: Susanna van Rose, writer and geologist

Library of Congress Cataloging-in-Publication Data

Harris, Nicholas.
Earthquakes through time / Nicholas Harris.
p. cm. — (Fast forward)
Includes index.
ISBN 978-1-4358-2803-2 (library binding)
1. Earthquakes—History—Juvenile literature. I. Title.
QE521.3.H247 2009
551.22—dc22

2008031651

Printed and bound in China

FAST FORWARD

Earthquakes
Through Time

illustrated by Peter Dennis
text by Nicholas Harris

PowerKiDS
press.

New York

Contents

4

Introduction

Imagine you are walking along a street in Japan. Suddenly, there is a great roar
and the ground starts to shake wildly beneath your feet. You are in
great danger! For the next few minutes, many things happen around you,
one following another with terrifying speed.
The story told in this book is like a journey. It is not a journey you can make
by plane, car or ship. In fact, you don't have to go anywhere at all. You are
about to travel through time. With each turn of the page, the time moves
forward a few seconds, hours or even years. Each new time—each stop on
your journey—is like a chapter in the story. The first wild shaking, the
tumbling of buildings, the cracks opening up in the ground, the caving in of
bridges, the landslide, the vast waves engulfing the shore, the fires sweeping
through the destroyed city, the rescue of people from beneath the rubble, the
building of a museum years later to record the events of those fateful moments
all tell the story of the great earthquake.

Use the thumb index to travel through time! This will help you make a quick comparison between one scene and another, even though some show events that took place many years apart. A little black arrow on the page points to the time of the scene illustrated on that page.

About 3,000 Years Ago...

It is late afternoon on the island of Honshu, Japan. A small band of hunters are returning to their village along the coast path. As they start to climb down through the woods, they are startled by a sudden loud, thundering noise.

Looking up, they see the cliff on the opposite side of the bay fall into the sea. Out in the water, they see waves start to rear up several feet (m) high and crash onto the shore. Their village, built on the flat land close to the water's edge, will be flooded. It is a horrifying sight.

The men know that an earthquake has struck. This is not an unusual event—small ground tremors lasting a few moments occur almost weekly—but no harm is caused. This quake is different. The men have never seen so much of the cliff fall before, nor witnessed such colossal waves.

WHAT IS AN EARTHQUAKE?

The outer layer of the Earth is made up of a number of giant slabs, called tectonic plates. These are always on the move. In some places, the edges are moving apart. In others, they are colliding, with one plate sliding underneath the other. In still others, one plate edge slides alongside another plate. This movement is very slow—about .5 inch (1 cm) a year—but the pressure is enormous. When plate edges grind against one another, they send out shock waves through the ground. We feel this as the shaking that is an earthquake.

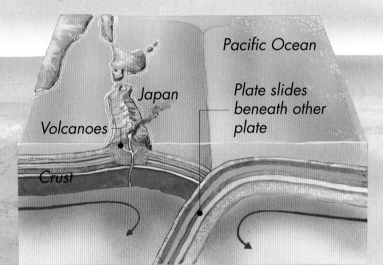

Pacific Ocean

Japan

Plate slides beneath other plate

Volcanoes

Crust

Most earthquakes are small tremors that do no harm. But when sliding plates lock together, pressure builds up in the rocks underground. Finally the pressure becomes too much for the rock to withstand. It snaps, causing a major earthquake.

The place where the rock breaks is called the focus of the earthquake. The point above it on the Earth's surface is termed the epicenter.

Japan suffers from many earthquakes because it is situated near plate boundaries. The Pacific Plate is sliding down beneath the Eurasian Plate.

1000 BC

100 years ago

A few years ago

Later that day

Seconds later

At the same time

A few minutes later

20 minutes later

A few minutes later

Several hours later

The next morning

Today

A Hundred Years Ago...

The village has grown over the years and has now become a wealthy city with a busy seaport. The streets are crowded with carts and rickshaws. Street sellers offer all kinds of things for sale, including food, clothing, clogs, lanterns and toys. Amid all the noise and activity, a funeral procession slowly winds its way through the crowds. In one of the buildings, a tea ceremony is being held.

Area of landslide

Funeral procession

Lamps

Lanterns

Rickshaw

Over the years, the city has suffered many earthquakes. Most have been far too weak for anybody to notice, although some stronger quakes have caused some minor damage to the city. The city's buildings have been constructed in a way that makes them very resistant to earthquake shaking. Walls are made of wood and, between rooms inside the houses, with paper. The wooden beams holding up the thatch roofs are tied with rice straw ropes.

Part of roof cut away

Tea ceremony

Toys

Clogs

Smoked fish

1000 BC

100 years ago

A few years ago

Later that day

Seconds later

At the same time

A few minutes later

20 minutes later

A few minutes later

Several hours later

The next morning

Today

Thousands of earthquakes occur every year, some of them major ones. But only when cities are affected is there great loss of life.

A Few Years Ago...

The city is a modern metropolis. Many of its older buildings have been demolished and multistory buildings built of steel and glass have been built in their place.

This morning the weather is unusually hot and humid. The fog

Inside apartment

rolling in from the sea has been slow to lift. Cars and buses take people to work along the city streets as usual, but today there is a strange feeling in the air. Animals, including seabirds and people's pet dogs, are restless. Some fishermen chat on the sidewalk.

Unusually, they have caught no fish at all that morning. Many report having seen strange lights in the sea fog earlier. One old man, who remembers witnessing very similar events many years ago, is in no doubt as to what all this means. He tells whomever will listen: there will be an earthquake soon.

Traditional building

1000 BC

100 years ago

A few years ago

Later that day

Seconds later

At the same time

A few minutes later

20 minutes later

A few minutes later

Several hours later

The next morning

Today

11

Seismographs measure the size of shock waves caused by an earthquake. The shaking is recorded by a pen on a piece of paper rolled over a drum.

Later That Day...

The old man is right. An earthquake strikes that very afternoon.

With a deafening roar, the whole city starts to shake wildly. Within seconds, large concrete pieces start to fall off the outsides of buildings

Burst pipe

and crash to the ground. Windows fall and smash on the sidewalk below. In some buildings, the walls fall outward, causing the concrete floors to collapse on top of one another like a pack of cards. Sirens sound amid the din of falling rubble. People dash out into the street, screaming in panic. As they do so, great cracks in the road's surface start to open up. Cars swerve to avoid the cracks and screech to a halt. Some collide with each other or smash into buildings. Water from burst pipes and underground drains pours out onto the streets. Electricity cables spark and crackle. Everywhere, there is chaos.

Collapsing building

1000 BC

100 years ago

A few years ago

Later that day

Seconds later

At the same time

A few minutes later

20 minutes later

A few minutes later

Several hours later

The next morning

Today

The Chinese invented this earthquake detector in AD 132. When shaken, a rod inside it swings and opens one of the dragons' mouths, sending a ball into a toad's mouth with a loud clang. It records the direction of the quake.

Seconds Later...

Inside an apartment, a family just sitting down to a meal find themselves being tossed around their kitchen. The rocking and shaking causes plates to tip out of cupboards, pots and pans to crash to the floor and even the furniture and electrical appliances to slide around the room. Cracks appear in the ceiling and lumps of plaster start to crash down amid clouds of dust.

The children scream. Their mother shouts to them to get under the table. Everyone is terrified. It feels like a sickening roller-coaster ride in which everything is breaking up around them.

UNSTABLE GROUND

When shock waves from an earthquake pass through solid rock, it is completely unaffected. But shock waves passing through sediment such as moist sand or gravel cause them to become almost like a liquid. This is called liquefaction. Buildings sink into the liquefied sediment and tip over. Mexico City was built on old lake sediment, so many buildings were badly damaged when an earthquake struck the region in 1985. The districts of San Francisco that were damaged in the 1989 quake had been built on top of debris from the 1906 earthquake that had been dumped in the waterfront area.

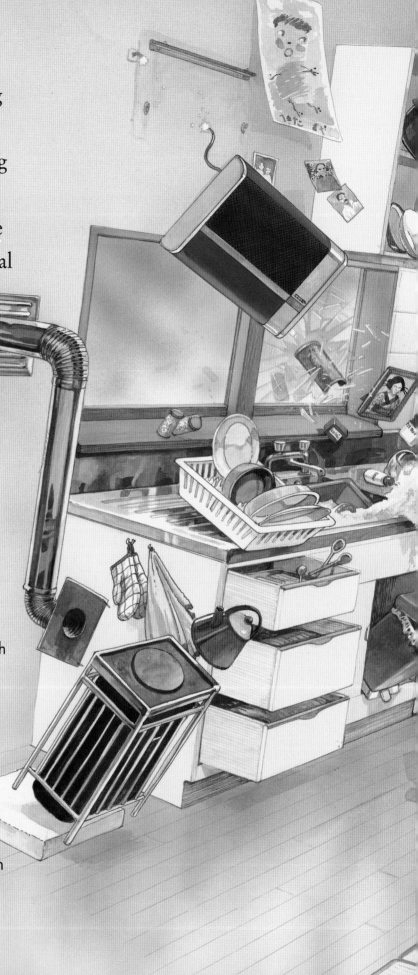

15

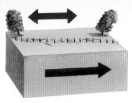

When rocks snap, two kinds of shock waves come out from the earthquake's focus. Primary (P) waves *(above)* press and stretch the rocks. Secondary (S) waves *(below)* shake them up and down and from side to side.

At the Same Time...

Just outside the city, farmers in the rice fields are thrown to the ground by the force of the earthquake. To the alarm of the terrified onlookers, the land itself rises and falls like the surface of the ocean as waves rush across it. In the fields, fountains of mud shoot into the air like miniature volcanoes. Cracks appear in the field and a nearby road folds, throwing cars off the edge.

Shock waves

Mud fountains

With a deafening crack, a railway bridge suddenly gives way as its concrete supports collapse. The tracks start to sag. The train driver hits his brakes hard in an attempt to stop his train from plunging to the ground.

Elevated railway

FAULTS

Rocks can bend and fold without breaking. Sometimes, when subjected to great pressure, they may suddenly break. The crack in the rocks where this sudden movement takes place is called a fault. As the pressure continues, rocks may move past one another along the same fault. During an earthquake, portions of land may be raised up or slip down along fault lines.

1000 BC

100 years ago

A few years ago

Later that day

Seconds later

At the same time

A few minutes later

20 minutes later

A few minutes later

Several hours later

The next morning

Today

17

These globes show where earthquakes occur around the world. Most take place at or near plate boundaries *(see page 7)*. The biggest are where plate edges slide alongside or where one slides under another.

A Few Minutes Later...

After 20 seconds the quake is over. But the terrible shuddering of the ground has not only caused buildings to collapse. Up on a hillside overlooking the city, the rocks and soil just beneath the surface have been made unstable by recent heavy rain. Now, sparked by the quake, the slope itself gives way. In a giant landslide, tons (t) of stones and soil, together with trees and shrubs, start to stream downhill. Houses, cars and anything else in the way of the landslide are carried along with it, adding to the slide. Alerted by the thunderous noise of falling rocks, people dash from their houses and run for their lives.

1000 BC

100 years ago

A few years ago

Later that day

Seconds later

At the same time

A few minutes later

20 minutes later

A few minutes later

Several hours later

The next morning

Today

19

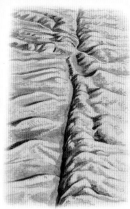

The San Andreas Fault stretches more than 750 miles (1,200 km) along the coast of California. It forms the boundary between two plates that are sliding past one another in opposite directions. The jerky movements result in constant, tiny shocks. Occasionally, pressure builds up over the years and is let out in a huge quake, such as the 1906 event in San Francisco.

Rescuing survivors

Finding survivors

Ambulance

Twenty Minutes Later...

During the quake, some people did not have time to escape before the buildings they were in collapsed. Miraculously, a few strong beams held up parts of the building in this street and saved people from being totally crushed. But they are now buried beneath piles of rubble. They have only dusty air to breathe and there is a risk that an aftershock (a lesser tremor that takes place after the main quake) will destroy their shelter. They cry out, hoping someone will rescue them quickly.

Soon, a crowd of helpers, including firefighters, emergency medical teams and some brave people who did manage to escape the falling buildings, rush to the scene. Listening for shouts of help, they lift away the rubble and cut through wood and twisted metal. Finally a loud cheer goes up as the first survivors are hauled to safety. They are carefully carried over the rubble to a waiting ambulance.

Just then, an aftershock causes the remains of the building to collapse. The rescuers were just in time!

1000 BC

100 years ago

A few years ago

Later that day

Seconds later

At the same time

A few minutes later

20 minutes later

A few minutes later

Several hours later

The next morning

Today

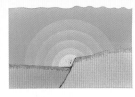

When the epicenter of an earthquake is on the seabed, a large underwater landslide can result *(above)*. This produces a series of fast-moving waves, traveling at around 500 miles per hour (800 km/h), called tsunamis (also known as tidal waves). In deep water, they are small, but as they approach the shallow coastal waters, they slow down and build up in height. Some tsunamis are many feet (m) high as they crash onto the shore *(below)*. The waves may last for several hours.

A Few Minutes Later...

On the sea coast, a group of people suddenly notice a huge wave out to sea, getting bigger all the time and rapidly moving toward them.

"Tsunami!" they yell, and everybody runs for their lives.

Soon, a wall of water some 100 feet (30 m) high appears. Ships and boats of all sizes are picked up and, as the giant wave rushes across the docks, are tossed

onto the shore. Many more tsunami waves follow, one after the other, over the next few hours. A hotel building on the sea shore escapes being destroyed by allowing the streams of water to pass through its lower floors.

TSUNAMIS

Tsunami is a Japanese word meaning "a wave breaking into a harbor." Most tsunamis are caused by earthquakes on the seabed. Some, sparked by quakes in one part of the world, do great harm to coastal areas a long way away. The great Chilean earthquake of May 1960 created tsunamis that destroyed Japan 10,000 miles (16,000 km) away.

23

1000 BC

100 years ago

A few years ago

Later that day

Seconds later

At the same time

A few minutes later

20 minutes later

A few minutes later

Several hours later

The next morning

Today

Night has fallen, but the effects of the earthquake are far from over. Fires have started. Sparked by fallen power lines and fed by gas escaping from broken gas

The Mercalli scale records the intensity of damage caused by an earthquake.
I-IV: Felt only by a few.
III-IV: Shaking as if by passing truck.

V: Buildings tremble, vases fall, trees shake.
VI: Bells ring, plaster cracks, people shaken.
VII: Loose tiles, old walls fall, chimneys crack.

VIII: Damage to buildings.
IX: Ground cracks, buildings collapse.
X: Landslides, bridges damaged, rails bent.
XI: Dams wrecked.
XII: Total devastation.

pipes, the flames quickly fan out among the stricken city's buildings. Moreover, broken water pipes make it very hard for the firefighters to put out the fires. Here they are using a pump to bring in water from other parts of the city where pipes are still intact. Elsewhere, they will need to blow up some buildings to stop the fire from spreading.

People who have been rescued from fallen buildings sit together in the street as the teams of firefighters attempt to save their homes from even further destruction. Meanwhile, rescue workers continue their search for survivors. They still have hopes that more people can be brought out from under the rubble. They will work on through the night.

Traditional building

25

1000 BC

100 years ago

A few years ago

Later that day

Seconds later

At the same time

A few minutes later

20 minutes later

A few minutes later

Several hours later

The next morning

Today

The Next Morning...

Dawn breaks on a scene of utter devastation. A reporter flies over the city in a helicopter, telling his shocked radio listeners what he can see below. Many buildings are damaged or totally destroyed. Large sections of the elevated roadway have fallen. Fire and flooding have laid waste to much of the city.

The Transamerica Building in San Francisco is built to withstand severe earthquakes. It is shaped like a slender pyramid and, thanks to its steel supports, its top is strong enough to sway 39 feet (12 m) and remain intact. In 1989 an earthquake shook California. Its epicenter was 60 miles (100 km) south of San Francisco. Although quite severe, the quake damaged few buildings in San Francisco. Most had been built to resist earthquake shaking.

Helicopter

Collapsed buildings

Collapsed roadway

But the story is not wholly gloomy. Many buildings, specially built to withstand earthquakes, have remained undamaged. They include a number of old buildings, with their wooden or paper walls and thatched roofs. And, despite the great ferocity of the quake, most of the city's inhabitants escaped harm. They have spent the night sleeping in tents. For the next few weeks, they will be without electricity and running water, but at least they are alive.

Fire-damaged buildings

Toppled building

Tents

27

1000 BC

100 years ago

A few years ago

Later that day

Seconds later

At the same time

A few minutes later

20 minutes later

A few minutes later

Several hours later

The next morning

Today

There are several ways in which buildings can be constructed to withstand severe quakes. Walls are anchored to concrete foundations reinforced with steel rods *(above)*.

Steel brackets anchor brick chimneys to the roof. Metal chimneys are lighter and safer.

Boilers are held in place by ties bolted to the wall, preventing gas pipes from breaking.

Steel connectors reinforce the joints between the wooden beams and joists supporting the floors and ceilings.

Video

Globe showing where earthquakes occur

Model of traditional house

Model of city struck by earthquake

Seismograph

Today, a Few Years Later

A party of schoolchildren is visiting a museum. It was built recently as a record of the terrible events of a few years ago, in which the city suffered its worst-ever earthquake.

The exhibits tell people all about earthquakes. There are models showing the Earth's plates and what a fault in the rocks looks like. The visitors watch a video of what happened during the quake in their city and look at a model of the immense damage it caused.

There are also exhibits that show how traditional houses were built to withstand earthquakes. A seismograph records small tremors as they actually happen in the city today.

Children try out an earthquake simulator. The floor shakes around, making it very hard for them to stand upright. The children have a lot of fun falling down, but their parents remember that when the real earthquake struck, the shaking was so terrible they feared for their lives.

Rebuilt city

Model of fault

Earthquake simulator

1000 BC

100 years ago

A few years ago

Later that day

Seconds later

At the same time

A few minutes later

20 minutes later

A few minutes later

Several hours later

The next morning

Today

Glossary

aftershock (AF-ter-shok) A lesser tremor that takes place after the main earthquake. There may be many aftershocks, sometimes continuing for months afterward.

crust (KRUST) The thin, rocky outer layer of the Earth.

debris (duh-BREE) The remains of something broken down or destroyed.

earthquake (URTH-kwayk) A shaking of the ground caused by the sudden movement of part of the Earth's crust. Earthquakes usually (but not always) occur at or near the boundaries of tectonic plates.

epicenter (EH-pih-sen-ter) The point on the Earth's surface directly above the focus of an earthquake.

fault (FAWLT) A crack in the Earth's surface produced when pressure from plate movements causes brittle rocks to break. The rocks move in opposite directions on either side of the fault, causing an earthquake.

focus (FOH-kis) The point in the Earth's crust where the rocks suddenly break, sending out shock waves.

foundations (fown-DAY-shunz) The bases of buildings constructed so that their weight is supported on firm ground or bedrock.

landslide (LAND-slyd) The sudden and rapid movement of soil and rock down a slope.

liquefaction (lih-kwuh-FAK-shun) The process by which moist sediments, when shock waves are passed through them, become almost like a liquid.

Mercalli scale (mer-KA-lee SKAYL) A measure of the intensity of damage caused by earthquake shaking, based on the effects on buildings and the landscape.

primary (P) wave (PRY-mer-ee WAYV) A shock wave that comes from the focus of an earthquake.

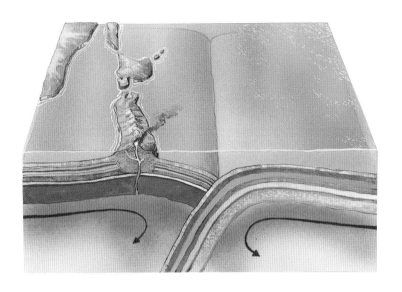

tectonic plates (tek-TAH-nik PLAYTS) The large pieces into which the Earth's surface is divided. Each plate moves slowly, either pushing into another plate, pulling away from it or sliding underneath it.

tremor (TREH-mur) A shaking of the ground.

tsunami (soo-NAH-mee) A sea wave caused by an earthquake occurring beneath the seabed.

volcanoes (vol-KAY-nohz) Openings in the surface of Earth that sometimes shoot up a hot liquid rock called lava.

P-waves cause the rocks to shake back and forth in the direction of wave movement.

secondary (S) wave (SEH-kun-der-ee WAYV) A shock wave that comes from the focus of an earthquake. S-waves cause the rocks to shake from side to side and up and down at right angles to the direction of wave movement.

sediment (SEH-deh-ment) Eroded rock pieces, such as sand and gravel, moved and laid down by wind, water or ice, usually in layers.

seismograph (SYZ-muh-graf) A device that makes a lasting record of earthquake shaking.

shock wave (SHOK WAYV) A wave of energy that comes from the focus of an earthquake. Also called a seismic wave.

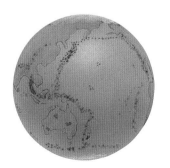

Index

Web Sites

Due to the changing nature of Internet links, PowerKids Press has developed an online list of Web sites related to the subject of this book. This site is updated regularly. Please use this link to access the list:
www.powerkidslinks.com/fastfor/quake/